FATHERS AND SONS

B.L. MAKIEFSKY

FATHERS AND SONS

2 STORIES

MISSION POINT PRESS

Published by Mission Point Press
2554 Chandler Rd.
Traverse City, MI 49696
(231) 421-9513
MissionPointPress.com

ISBN: 978-1-954786-77-6
Printed in the United States of America

CONTENTS

THE LONG RUN
9

SNOW COUNTRY
25

AKNOWLEDGMENTS
38

ABOUT THE AUTHOR
39

THE LONG RUN

"COOLER BY THE LAKE" was no longer heard on the evening news, and in the sunbaked hills that ringed town, the cherries—normally at market by now—clung to the trees like peas. Three months of drought and unprecedented heat had shallowed Grand Traverse Bay, leaving it bathtub warm, warmer in July than the locals could remember, and the fruit had suffered for it. Still, the celebration of the harvest would go on. As would the runner, Merrit Reef.

Townsfolk and tourists toting lawn chairs and coolers trickled downtown this Saturday morning, more to watch the festival parade than the half-marathon. "A good day to race," said an older man in black knee socks. "A good day to die," said another.

"Forget personal bests," bullhorned an official above the din. "Today you run to survive."

Reef, age thirty and a strong runner, would take his chances. He moved towards the starting line and watched the high school marching bands warming up, strutting past floats that hummed or belched, fairylands and volcanoes, tree houses and dragons. Young festival queens—apple, asparagus, trout, and cherry, of course—stood fanning themselves in the beds of pickups or front seats of convertibles.

A distant trumpet played with Reef's heart: slow, haunting notes that drifted overhead like embers in the hot and thick air. Something that his father would sing? He wasn't sure. His father loved a good parade. He'd hum and clap and whistle at every float that went by.

The sweet smells of cotton candy and buñuelos (elephant ears) hung in the air as well. Men on stilts juggled rosy bouquets and long steely knives as a young boy shouted from his father's shoulders. Seagulls, whiter than the white sun, skimmed the blue-green surf at the marina. A long, tube-like balloon, dressed as a sausage in running shorts and Nikes, stirred in the slightest of breezes, kite-like, then settled down in the flatbed truck where it was moored.

"Hey, Reef!" shouted Mark Silver, his training partner. "Faster than last year?"

A year ago the cherries were on time and Reef, exhausted from working double shifts at the cannery, had overslept and missed the race. But today would be different. He had set two alarms and gone to bed early. He dreamt—and it was the same dream most nights the past year—that he outkicked his nearest rival at the finish, took first place in his age bracket and got his picture in the Sunday paper. In this dream, Reef was kissed by the festival queen, and he'd awake feeling the cool trophy in his sweaty palm.

Today, on the thirtieth running of the Cherry Festival Half-Marathon, an event that *Runner's World* had called—as much for the heat as for the poorly marked trail—"a summer rite of passage," Merrit Reef had something to prove. The parade was not going to pass him by.

"See you at the podium," he said to Silver.

The runners, smelling of sunscreen and sweat, edged closer to the starting line. Reef took a deep breath. The furnace-like air did not yet singe his lungs.

"One minute," bellowed the starter.

Reef eyed the competition left and right: All perched as one, a wild and frantic knot of anticipation strung together by nerves, will, and hope; the same hands-on-watches lean, the slow and the fast, practiced and new, young and old; the same hunger to do well. The man in black knee socks wished him luck. Reef smiled, retied his laces, and then turned to face the Jack-in-the-packs behind him, the jog trotters and expansive women in spandex he trained so desperately to stay ahead of.

The countdown started and the chorus of onlookers shouted words of encouragement over the staccato-like drills of the parade's Briefcase Brigade, the Wall Street pretenders strutting down Main Street.

Waiting for the gun, Reef again heard horns, a tuba even, and the same broken melody, slow and familiar. Time stood still, although he nevertheless heard it counted.

And—bang! A thread was pulled, the knot unraveled, the horses let loose from the barn. A flurry of arms and legs stampeded past Reef.

Easy now, he told himself. Only children, dogs, and fools sprinted the first mile of a long race. *They'll "come back"—or get lost in the woods,* Reef chuckled to himself as the runners turned toward the shore like a centipede six blocks long.

Easy now. Each foot strike, like some race day mantra, tapped the familiar words. Don't go out too hard. *Easy now.*

Relaxed and cheerful, he watched sailboats leave the harbor toward an endlessly blue horizon. "Six minutes and ten seconds," announced the timekeeper at mile one, as the wave of runners pushed on. *Too fast. Easy now.*

At three miles the lead pack, which Reef was a part of, climbed above downtown as the long string of runners trailed in pursuit. Overcome by heat, a few left the marked route, stepped over a guardrail, and scampered down the embankment to plunge pell-mell into the bay. *Quitters.* As he followed the turn and crested the hill, he saw the Ferris wheel and the sun's glare on the painted capsules of other amusements that catapulted riders into space. Far past the Midway, a red construction crane was suspended above the hospital, and beyond that the forest marked the horizon with a dark and uneven line. Reef knew it was there where the race would be won, or lost.

"Do you believe it?" said Mark Silver, now at Reef's side. He pointed to what looked like a wayward missile darting across the bay.

Reef tried to make sense of it. "The sausage tied to the truck?"

"Not anymore."

Eager to explore new markets, farmers were promoting a cherry-flavored sausage in the parade.

"Fast food for sure," said Reef. "Let's hope for a happy landing."

"An argument to run under control," said Silver as he surged ahead, his mop of dark hair flapping with each foot strike.

"You know I'm going to medal," Reef said, shaking off early fatigue to match the reedlike Silver stride for stride. "Maybe even take yours."

The two friends often bantered like that on their runs, emitting small talk, like sonar, to gauge the other's strength. Now Silver, a few years older than Reef, laughed. "At what price? Running your 100-mile weeks?" Silver grabbed a water in stride at the five-mile aid station. "I know you," he said to Reef. "I know that you run to work. And work to run." He drained the cup and discarded it. "And that you probably run in your dreams, too." He found Reef's hand and briefly squeezed it before letting go. "I know that when you, Merrit Reef, imagine what you can least live without, sweat is the last to go."

"What are you saying?"

"Life is more than a personal best."

"Maybe so," said Reef. He thought of their last run together, a Friday in June after his shift ended, their footsteps almost imperceptible on the soft dirt trail as they looped back to Silver's farm. Moonlight had settled over the pasture like chalk dust and the song of whip-poor-wills rose from all corners. The evening filled Reef with joy and purpose.

Silver, a reporter for the *Bear County Almanac*, made Reef feel less self-conscious about working at the cannery, where his world followed a seasonal axis of asparagus, strawberries, cherries, peas (which they processed for Gerber's), squash, and apples. Whatever crop came down the line, and whatever money he could raise himself for the three Rs: rent, running shoes, and race fees. "Merrit the Carrot," others teased him at work. The elements had weathered him as surely as if he had gone to sea: a bone-deep tan, sun-bleached hair (sometimes white) and, as if deep-fried, eyebrows the color of orange peels. The older Hispanic women rolled their eyes when at shift's end he hit the ground running, and the younger ones smiled as he darted past. They laughed at him in two languages and went home to large families in small trailers that dotted the orchards.

Though Reef lived alone, the hour (or three) he ran daily felt, and bewilderingly so, like the only one that was his. Running gave him that: time, paradoxically, to stop and think. Time to celebrate the flesh, a body so finely tuned it would endure great hardship and call it pleasure; time enough—and the longer the distance, the clearer the view—to see also what he had left behind: his accounting degree. And his father, who had paid for it.

Now as Reef tucked in behind Silver at the eight-mile mark of the race, he thought—the way random thoughts come on the move, though they are hardly random—that a long run wasn't unlike his relationship with his father. An uneasy comfort. Each pushed him places he was reluctant to go. His father wasn't doing well, and Reef had put off seeing him. Maybe he'd go after the race, he told himself. He'd go after cherries, that was it. It would be a short crop, maybe last a week or so. They could settle their differences then. A bushel full of hurt.

The two were as different as a father and son could be. Merrit Sr., a plumber from Grand Rapids, outgoing, humming and whistling his way through life. And the shy Reef, running from his own skin. Nothing about his father even fit, thought Reef. Broad shoulders and bandy legs. The oversized head, as round and bald as a cue ball. That small, tight mouth nevertheless able to swallow whole any praise before it escaped his lips. Delicate hands. The absurd nickname: *Ritty.*

Reef was taller than his father, too, and it had always seemed so. At school classmates called him *Jack* or *Beanstalk* so he turned inward, away from the jitter of nervous adulation and freakish slurs. There was one voice, however, that he couldn't turn away, and it rang clear as a bell. *Run far,* it said. *Run often.* He followed that call. There would be sightings of Reef all over the city. He ran to school and to his father's shop, to the library or dentist, and on errands for his mother. Sweat became his life's blood; a day without running was a day consigned to shadows. At night in bed he continued the dance, and his legs twitched urging him on.

The markers Reef passed, however, were never as clear or better or more pure as the ones just ahead. Still, the motion and repetition of running allowed him to sort the music from the dissonance. That was his song: a road, and the will to follow it.

"SEVENTY-ONE MINUTES!" shouted the timekeeper at the ten-mile mark. Reef grimaced.

FALL, THE PREVIOUS YEAR. Reef watched Ritty's pickup pull into his driveway. Festive shouts from the orchard across the road had pierced the damp and cool air as workers picked the last of the early apples. The truck's window was open and Reef heard his father whistling an old tune that Ritty had once made up his own lyrics to. Reef had forgotten the words, but at the time he and his sister laughed plenty. Now Ritty brought with him a new hot water tank. He turned off the truck engine and without any other words but "hello, son," sliced open the carton in the back of the truck with a razor-sharp pocketknife, its black casing worn smooth as a pebble. His father bore most of the tank's weight as the two men came up the porch stairs and into the kitchen. Ritty squared his shoulders at the door to the basement to align the load. He was still strong then.

Ritty hummed while he worked as his son handed the tools over. Reef thought of the other jobs he had helped his father on, and how he had once sawed a hole in the wrong spot in the sub-floor of a new house, halfway across the room. Not even close to where he was told to cut it. His father wasn't angry. "Don't sweat the small stuff," Ritty had laughed. "Just make it right. It's the same stinking shit." He fixed the hole like magic, hands working deftly to smooth things over. A part of Reef never forgot that moment, never forgot the desire to be by his father's side. To come back to the shop together, wrapped in that familiar smell of cigar smoke and machine oil. The smell of acceptance. Confidence. Love.

In the dank air of Reef's basement his father's torch flickered. Ritty bent over to cough and dropped a wrench. It clanked off a pipe and Reef shuddered.

When they finished his father said, "You probably want to go for a run."

"No," Reef said. "I ran this morning."

"Give it another ten minutes and you can shower," said Ritty, scrubbing his hands at the kitchen sink in cold, sudsy water. "It's a good model. I picked it up at the warehouse yesterday." Reef tried to pay his father. "Don't bother with that," said Ritty. Turning to go, he added, "You can't find anything better than canning peas?"

"If richer meant faster," Reef said, "I'd be all for it."

"I did whatever I could for you to be something," said his father, a hand on the door.

Reef stood his ground. "I'm a runner."

"What does that even mean? A runner."

Reef's heart pounded in his chest and his thoughts raced to the trails above Lake Michigan. To abandoned farms and hidden streams, to the scent of apple blossoms in May and the marsh at dusk where the trill of spring peepers had made him want to cry out over the mellifluous din that crowded his every heartbeat. To solitary winter mornings when he was the first to blaze a trail in the fresh snow that had blanketed his quiet village overnight. *Out the door is an open sea*, he wanted to scream at his father. *And every day I fish my limit.*

"I'm not good enough," he said. "Is that it?"

A gentle rain fell outside, and the kitchen windows had fogged up. Ritty stood in his ragged blue parka. His hand, as smooth and bright as porcelain, rested on the doorknob. Fine red lines, trellis-like, strained to hold back a sadness and discontent in his flecked brown eyes; a weariness that begged to be redeemed.

"What would you have me say?"

Reef wanted to hear him say that he missed and loved his boy.

"I don't care," said Reef. "Forget it."

REEF PICKED UP THE PACE and reeled Silver in as the trail corkscrewed up the side of a hill and into the shade. "Hey! Don't go getting lost," Silver said. "You'll miss the awards."

"I don't mind the woods," said Reef. "It cools you some."

"Maybe too much," said Silver.

They each grabbed a water from the aid stand at a clearing, but Reef's mostly spilled. "Come on!" shouted Silver. "Let's go!" Pass someone uphill, Reef knew, and you never had to look back. The edge was mental toughness. Not to let anyone as good as you prove they were better. Silver took off, Reef in tow. No one followed. But then Silver found yet another gear and pulled away. Or Reef had slowed. He wasn't sure. He struggled to maintain pace on the soft terrain. He had counted the miles but failed to consider the toll that his fast early splits would later exact. He regretted the water stops he skipped. He regretted a lot of things.

Now his thighs felt made of glass. Each painful landing, however soft, seemed to shatter something more. He jogged on the best he could and thought he saw Silver's bright racing singlet ahead—or was it a whitetail deer that flagged across the trail? The older man in black knee socks passed Reef as if he were a mere ghost, marching in place. The trail markers were fewer now.

Reef sat down on the felled trunk of a large beech tree, and the cool bark felt good against his throbbing hamstrings. This was new ground; he had never once stopped or walked in a race before, much less sat. Not knowing what else to do, he got back on his feet—but couldn't find the trail.

Where he last saw Silver he encountered a thicket of sumac, the red berries pale and drooping. He listened for other runners, but the woods were still as if the heat had choked the life from them. Not even a fly buzzed. The small clearing and the stand of water cups had vanished, too. He felt the forest close around him. Once on pace to a personal best and age group medal, Reef now shuffled about aimlessly, dehydrated and lost. The air burned yet the forest darkened as he pawed his way through it, searching for a way out.

For a deep, lost moment he saw himself shopping in a forgotten city after hours. The reflection of an ordinary man in the cold and empty storefront windows at first reassured him: he was not a ghost. He lived. But if it were him, why was he in running shorts? And—still looking at his reflection—how would he pay for what he wanted? He had no wallet, only a number. He went to try a door. It was locked tight, not even a rattle. On another he saw a sign: "Enter Here." And not until this door, too, failed to open did Reef let go of the tree branch he was clinging to, and remember that he was in the woods above the bay and thirsty as hell.

He then stumbled onto a tunnel-like path thick with pine needles, where old growth from the trees on each side had merged above him. Far ahead a light flickered. *Daylight*, he thought, and he pushed himself toward it, over roots, through the tangle and deadfall. And though the light, a beacon to him, didn't appear closer, without reason Reef filled with the vague and feverish sense that he was richer for the chase. Finally, through an opening in the dense cover, he saw more fully the shaft of light, a reflection off the crane that towered above the hospital below. He moved in that direction, through the dry high grass and thistle and down a narrow deer path etched into the hillside above a small parking lot. He placed one drunken foot in front of the other. In its essence, running was just a controlled fall; didn't George Sheehan say that? The trick now, he told himself, was to fall forward.

Pavement felt good after the uncertainty of the woods. Reef watched, mesmerized, as wisps of steam curled and rose from his racing flats. Inexplicably something grazed his head. He swatted at it as if to ward off a mosquito, then looked up to see the parade balloon with the oversized Nikes dangling above him. The sausage plummeted and Reef tripped over its spindly legs. It now lay on top of him, heavier than he had imagined, brushing his lips, sticking to his wet body like a lover.

"You fucking clown!" Reef screamed at the sausage. "Get off!"

A car door shut. From the pavement where he lay beneath the balloon Reef watched a young woman huffing two small children past him toward the hospital.

"Don't look!" the woman barked at the boy and girl. "*In the parking lot!*" she sneered at Reef. "Take your *friend* here and crawl back into to the woods or I'll call the police." She raised her purse above her head as if to strike him with it.

Reef thought that crawling might be a good thing, and wished he had thought of it sooner. Instead he got to his feet, grabbed the inflatable by the neck, and in one furious blow of almost all that was left of his strength, he struck the balloon squarely in the gut. He watched it sail away, kicking its legs high to what looked like a Mexican hat dance.

Reef tried to establish a rhythm. *Easy now*, he repeated again and again, but his feet just didn't get it. They more or less slapped the ground, like fish out of water. He found a side door to the hospital open. The drinking fountain was past the emergency room entrance where, displaced by the new construction, a few beds lined the wall. Reef leaned hard with both hands on the cool steel as he bent over to drink.

"Son, is that you?"

Reef waited, head down, drinking deeply, for the voice, and man, to disappear. For someone else to answer. When no one did he glanced over to see his father clear as day, sitting upright in a hospital bed. In disbelief Reef stepped closer and strained to see the name fastened to the patient's wrist. But the older man folded his thick arms.

"Merrit, you look like hell. What happened?"

The two stared at each other. "A long run, Dad," Reef finally said. "And you? What are you doing here? Did your doctor—"

"Doesn't matter much," he laughed. "Same stinking shit."

"Is anyone with you?"

"I'm good. Got a nice view of the bay here."

Reef looked around. The bed was crammed into a dim corridor and there were no windows in sight.

"You in the parade, son?"

"Not this one," said Reef.

"Too bad," said the old man. "You know I like a good parade."

"Can we talk after the race?" Reef said. "I'd better go. I have some catching up to do."

"We both do," said his father. "We both do." He coughed, and put his hand in the air, as if to ask for Reef to wait. "Son?" he said after a minute.

"What?"

"Did you fish your limit out there today?" His hand, still overhead, turned into a fist and shook with a genuine enthusiasm. The inside of the hospital was a good twenty degrees cooler than the street, and Reef started to shake. "Merrit?"

"Yes?" Reef was halfway to the exit.

"Go easy now, son."

YOU NEVER KNOW, thought Reef as he reentered the half-marathon not far from the hospital's main entrance. *You hear one thing, then another. Maybe his doctor's here now. I'll talk to them both after the race.* He grabbed a water at the twelve-mile mark to soak his throbbing head.

He thought he saw Mark Silver ahead. With an adrenaline-fueled surge of joy, he reached out to him. And yet—with his hand on his fellow runner's shoulder—anger instead erupted. "It isn't sweat that you can least live without," Reef screamed. "It's love! It's love!"

The runner (and several others) turned around, puzzled.

"I'm sorry," muttered Reef. "I thought you were my friend."

Reef tailed the last of the runners towards the finish as they dodged festivalgoers darting here and there to watch the parade. Latecomers tugged on their children's hands, as vendors hawked cups brimming with cherries from Washington. Reef found himself in the midst of the Briefcase Brigade, the dozen or so men dressed alike in dark suits who parodied corporate life. They marched in tight circles as fast as he could run, and up close he saw that their suits were threadbare, their breast-pocket handkerchiefs stained, expensive leather shoes old and worn. He felt beaten down and wanted to cry.

Music exploded from all sides now as marching bands converged on Front Street. Reef separated himself from the brigade and the briefcases clicked endlessly behind him, like the shutters of a thousand cameras. He caught up to a large woman, her racing bib reduced to postage-stamp size by her massive frame. He had no strength left to pass her. Two young boys in the crowd along the curb jumped up and down on fresh legs, shouting to the woman. "Mom! You're ahead of Merrit the Carrot! Mom! Merrit the Carrot!"

The woman turned to see what the fuss was about, and Reef recognized Trudy from the cannery. "Hello, love," she said warmly. "You can do it."

Trudy's heart was as big as she was wide. She called everyone "love," and said she was raised in England, but someone at work told Reef that Trudy was born and raised in Bear County and had never once left. She wore black capri tights with lime-green stripes and a large sweatshirt to cover her girth. Still, she appeared much less fatigued than Merrit Reef. Even her long dark hair remained perfectly braided.

"I know you hurt, love," she said to him. "But you can do it."

Her boys cheered, "Go, Mom, go!" They jumped up and down, buzz cuts pogoing above the sea of faces curbside.

Reef saw Mark Silver past the finish line clutching his medal and talking to a race official. They were looking his way. Reef moved, or was moved, surrounded yet lost—a speck of dust in a pool of molasses—and suddenly he was at ease, out of his body, soaring above the masses and music. Town spread out like a set of toys beneath him. He saw the band shell, and empty park benches. Lifeguards. He saw friends and family. Strangers with love in their hearts. Balloons.

He couldn't tell whether he was floating towards the finish or merely higher, and he wasn't sure it mattered. His thoughts spiraled into a yin and yang. The sky, and bay. Life and death. War and peace. Time, immeasurable. The ticking of a clock from somewhere deep. His journey seemed endless and he felt remarkably whole, as if he were higher than a kite and had witnessed a glorious sunset to a perfect day.

He felt the ground slam into him hard. His ears popped like cap guns. *Bang. Bang.*

Trudy looked at him, smiling, moving as steadily as a tank.

Now Reef heard horns playing the familiar melody, the one that had haunted him at the start of the race. Yes, his father would sing it when he went with him mornings to the wholesaler to pick up supplies. Yes, that was it. That goddamn stupid song. *The Farmer in the Dell!* Only Ritty had changed the words. *The Plumber in the Well,* he would sing. *The plumber takes a son /*

The son takes a run / Hi-ho, the derry-o / The plumber takes a son. Reef's legs would not much move, but his heart soared.

"Come on now, love," Trudy said at Reef's side. "We're almost there." Reef stumbled but she caught him by the hand and raised it triumphantly as the two crossed under the finish line banner. He held on tight.

"MERRIT, I'M...SORRY," said Mark Silver, helping the spent Reef to his feet.

"For what? I got disoriented. I hit the wall and flipped out. Hugging a fucking tree." He grabbed a cup of sweet cherries from the refreshments offered runners. "I remember shopping! For what, goddamn it? Shoes? A way out? And then Trudy—Trudy!"

"No, no...your sister. She's been trying to reach you," said Silver, his voice cracking. "I'm so sorry." Tears rolled down his sweat-caked face. "Your father..." Silver could not finish the sentence. A white Cutlass convertible turned the corner inches from them, and in the back seat alongside the festival queen from Kalkaska perched a trout ten feet tall with rainbow scales that looked impossibly wet.

"They tried to find you on the course," Silver said. "They even paged you, here at the finish."

Reef started to walk away.

"Merrit. Where are you going?"

"The hospital. I saw him there."

"No, you don't understand," said Silver, catching up to Reef and blocking his path. "Your sister is home. Your father died there. In Grand Rapids. Earlier this morning."

"Grand Rapids."

Silver nodded. "They took him to emergency. She couldn't reach you."

Reef turned to look at the sailboats across the bay. The music started to fade and the hot air pushed down on him so that he was unable to breathe or talk. But still—his heart went on, crazily—then slowly, and in that void between the beats was a gap wide enough for the parade to start and the parade to end. *Grand Rapids? But I saw him. Things don't matter much, he said.* Reef was scared and frozen, his wet singlet sticking to him like paste.

Silver put an arm around Reef and steered him toward the car. *Easy now.*

Easy now.

SNOW COUNTRY

MARK SILVER peered through his truck's windshield this snowy December afternoon, trying to find his way. Whiteouts swept over the pickup and he floated, a cloud among clouds, pulled forward blindly as if to a hitch in a carwash. When the snow finally let up he turned off the radio ("Do You Hear What I Hear") and stepped outside to figure out where he was. *At least I'm on a road,* he thought, seeing the misty outline of trees only yards from his truck door. He drove on cautiously, passing bleak fields of what had been corn or squash, and not until he climbed a steep hill above the town of Sears Harbor did he know the road he travelled. Winter was like that along the Lake Michigan shore—at times you needed a plow or snowmobile, maybe both—but the skiing was good, and Mark thought that if what was good was also important in your life, then you were well off.

He wandered in and out of the aisles at the market, grabbed a few things, and chatted with the cashier before walking slowly back to his truck. Town smelled of cut pine, road salt, and gasoline from the handful of snowmobiles squatting in front of Walker's Bar. Vendors selling wreaths and trees mostly ignored Mark and that suited him just fine. Here and there, he heard the scrape of a shovel and the splitting of wood. The bells from St. Vincent's Church tolled softly in the fog of snow. Small lights burned from storefront awnings, blinking like portholes in vast and snow-covered hulls. Afternoon faded into dusk.

"Silver. Merry Christmas. Got your tree up?" Eddie Brandon, who ran his family's Christmas tree farm, startled him.

"No, guess I don't," Mark said.

"I got one for you. About giving them away at this point." Eddie was short with a sharp beak for a nose and he stood there in his Carhartts without hat or gloves, snow filling his shaggy blond hair and beard like fine sugar.

Mark looked at the fir trees leaning against the hardware store, which the Brandons also owned. They seemed freakish to him, limp and meager. "Not this time," he said. "But thanks."

"Hell and tarnation, Silver, how do you do without a tree? You leaving town?" Mark shook his head. "Then I'm giving you one. I know you ain't working now." He went to grab a tree. "Where you parked?"

"Ah, thanks again. But same answer."

"Silver! Unless you cut your own, you won't find a better deal. It's free. Free!"

Mark shifted the weight of his bag. Eddie, however, misunderstood the gesture, and thought Mark was handing him the groceries to carry the tree himself.

"I can take that for sure," said Eddie, reaching for the bag and giving Mark the tree.

"Please," said Mark. "I don't want it."

Eddie put the tree down. Beads of ice were frozen to the ends of his eyelashes, stuck there like spider eggs. "I don't get it. You one of them Je—"

"—Gypsies?" said Mark, his throat tightening.

"Yeah, Gypsies," Eddie said, nodding.

"Something like that," said Mark.

"I'll be," said Eddie. "The whole family?"

"As long as I remember."

"That so?" Eddie said, his blue eyes probing Mark's face. "We'll say a prayer for you." He shook his head and turned his back to look up the street.

Mark got back to his truck and exhaled. Leaving Sears Harbor, he followed a county plow until it turned on the state highway to Pentwater. He was on his own. The snow fell in great strips now, like pieces of ragged linen, and his wipers, lurching back and forth, screeched into the quiet, trying to make a difference. Fifty yards from the house he lost control of the truck, slid harmlessly into a drift by the creek, and from there had to go on foot. The snow was deep, but light, and he followed a deer trail until it cut back into the woods. Sarita waited for him on the porch, snow like stardust in her long black hair.

"Do you need help carrying it?" she asked. She started to call for her son Jesse but stopped. "Will you be going back out?"

"Can't see a thing out there," said Mark. He brushed himself off and carried the one bag of groceries inside. She followed him to the fireplace, where he tossed in a chunk of wood, took the poker and arranged the logs just so. Mark knew nothing about Christmas trees, even less about the wanting of them, but he had found solid reasons for rejecting those that were left. Free or not. "They weren't any good," he said.

"I'm glad you're back safe," said Sarita. "Safe isn't the same as okay, is it?"

"I'm fine," Mark said, not turning around, mashing the logs about and staring at the rising flames. One lie fueled the next. "There's time. You'll see."

"Time for what?" she said.

Twelve-year old Jesse stood at the top of the stairway. The angle gave strength to his slight frame.

"It isn't so bad," said Mark.

"The weather? It's worse than bad," Sarita said. "It snows every day here." She grabbed the fire poker and playfully nudged him. "Or did you mean Christmas?"

Jesse raced down the stairs. "Why didn't you bring a tree?"

"Does it matter?" asked Mark.

"What do you mean?" said Sarita.

"Christmas goes on, doesn't it? Do you really need lights and trees and all that stuff?" He didn't mean for it to come out that way. He went to the window and watched it fill with snow, like an hourglass with sand. He shut his eyes tight, and still it came down. Christmas made him want to burrow underground like a mole, and come out when it passed. Mark Silver had always looked upon the holidays as King Solomon did upon the bereaved and contentious mothers: You go for one or the other. You had to shake the pretender out. What made him think that he could celebrate Christmas?

He had left Sears Harbor with odds and ends, not with what he told Sarita and Jesse he'd bring home—today, yesterday, and for the past two weeks. Silver, thirty-two years old, had plenty of time these days. He was laid off from the *Bear County Almanac,* where he reported agricultural news and events; farmers didn't have much to say in winter. This last trip to town he'd gotten back to the pickup with his heart pounding—and he didn't even know what he had paid for. Now the snow came down faster than the plows could push it back, and the road would be drifted shut. Going back would be impossible, maybe for days.

"Why!" The boy repeated, circling Mark as if he were prey. For a time the three of them had lived in one of those snow-white paperweight worlds. Only now he wished someone would just stop shaking it. Wished she hadn't turned his world upside down. He'd been looking for someone to share expenses and Sarita, too, was out of work.

"Jesse! Enough." Sarita steered him out of the room. He stepped around her. "We always have a tree!" Jesse yelled. "At least we used to." He added something in Spanish and his mother said to stop that right now.

"Jesse doesn't think he'll get anything without a tree," said Sarita, returning.

But they knew better. Gifts had come, from the great aunt and cousins in Chicago, her father and sister in Donna, Texas. The boy even signed for one himself. And with his first unemployment check, Mark had bought Jesse skis, not new ones, but used wooden ones that smelled of pine tar and wax and still had slow turns in deep powder left in them. He gave them to him the first good snow after Thanksgiving.

Mark and Sarita stood face-to-face, loosely holding hands. She was almost as tall as his six feet, with broad shoulders and a darkly handsome face that her easy smile filled. Her eyes were black pools of resolve or devotion or desire—Mark was never sure which. She wore two pairs of jeans to keep warm (the second ones, the overalls, were his), and a wool sweater from the Goodwill. She smelled of coarse soap, not perfume, and fresh cut apples—the same as when he had interviewed her for the *Almanac*, after Jesse's accident. She told him then her real name was Esperanza, but to call her Sarita. She said that she had stopped using Esperanza when her mother died. He reported that, too.

His articles about the hard work and hard knocks of the road-weary migrant mother and son were picked up by the AP wire. After the story—and harvest—ran its course, he offered them a place to stay.

"Farmers tell me that all the time," she had said.

"What do you tell them?"

"That my work is in the field. And stays there. If you want something more, go to Fred's List."

"I think you mean *Craigslist*," said Mark.

"*Lo mismo*," she said. "Fred or Craig. You see what I mean."

"I'm not a farmer," Mark told her. "But I grow things just the same, and put them down on paper." He thought of the stories and novel that he would write during his layoff.

"So how many families does this paper of yours feed?" she asked.

He didn't have an answer then, and he didn't have one now.

Over her shoulder, in the yard where the kitchen lights fell, was a sea of white. Night came swiftly in the woods beyond. Mark yearned to join the storm outside, stark forests, heavy squalls, snow so frequent it never soiled. The world of black and white that he knew best. He squeezed her hands and turned away.

Sarita unpacked the groceries: flour, coffee, bagels, soy milk, shampoo, the *Detroit Free Press*. She already had what they needed to make a special dinner. "You go for a tree and bring this?" Her words were not unkind. They never were. "What were you thinking?"

"That I don't celebrate Christmas," Mark said. He saw Jesse's face in the doorway.

Sarita said nothing.

Mark went to the window—five inches of snow or twenty, what did it matter to her? After the first two her old beater car with the bad tires never got her anywhere anyway. But he would give her the truck if she wanted to leave. She knew that. When the lake first gave up the heavy clouds, they stayed up nights talking as the squalls drifted inland, wave after wave of snow that by morning clung like thick cotton to the black willows that surrounded his rented farmhouse. She told him that in Texas the heat came so fast and early in the year that those going north were considered lucky. But staying past fall? Unlucky. But maybe, just maybe, okay, she had said, smiling at him. She said she'd stay until Jesse—who had been in an accident at the cannery—was feeling stronger. On Mark's first day home on layoff he overheard her talking on the phone. "*No es amor, ni el ambiente, ni Mark Silver,*" he thought she said. Her words echoed loudly in the large house and his heart sank, though he wasn't sure of the Spanish. "It's a good house," she said. "Colder than *El Valle* but warmer than the migrant camp." Of course it would be nice to be home for Christmas, she said. But they would see what it would bring, winter in this place.

Now the phone rang. Sarita, expecting a call from Texas, answered and passed it to Mark.

"Who was that?" his mother asked.

"Sarita. A friend."

"That's an odd name."

"Not around here."

His mother hesitated like a car caught between gears. Mark sensed that she wanted to go somewhere, say something, but was stalled. He pictured her in her red leather jacket, its collar turned up against the cold, driving in Detroit on dry pavement yet trying hard to steer clear of drifts of one sort or another. "What happened to the nice woman you wrote about?" she finally said. "Did she make it home?"

"Sarita and her son are staying at the farm. We're snowed in."

"Oh," she said, as if nothing had been said at all. "Will you be coming home soon?"

"It's a long way back," Mark said.

MARK SLEPT POORLY that night. He moved from dream to dream, treading here, forced there, each step closer to a side he could sense and never reach, as if he were crossing a fierce river and there was no return.

Snow filled his bedroom with sand.

He saw his mother, lurching in that space between gears.

Voices scratched at his window, like sleet.

He was frightened and tried to run but his blankets gathered like drifts, pinning him down. Then he saw himself at Sarita's door. The snow fell all around him now, and he called out to her. *If only I had my skis.* Then he was flying, really flying, carving turns around the black holes and bright constellations of his dream. He skied the planets and the stars, the sun and the moon, and along the Milky Way. But suddenly in this frenzy of space the snow gave way to ice and he plunged head over heels, out of control, his face peeled back like a mask on the barren, windswept slope. He got up, fell, and rose again, each time with a new face, a new mask. Finally, he stayed upright and brushed himself off. He wasn't hurt, but something was wrong: He could not find his way back. In anger, he raised his fist to the heavens. And the stars with their thousand faces laughed. Again he called her name. Esperanza.

Fully awake, Mark dressed and went outside into the night. The wind had shifted away from the lake, and with it the storm's fury. As the last of the dark clouds overhead broke up, the new snow glittered like diamonds. The cold that braced him failed to still his doubts. How did you give, without giving up? He listened to the now swollen creek that ringed the farm, as if an answer could somehow be plucked from it.

The snow was deep but light. The skiing would be very good. The only sounds were his heart and the quickness of the creek. Across the pasture and above the tall spruces by the highway, the gay lights strung on Miles VanSlyke's silo twinkled like distant stars.

He got the skis out, brushed himself off, reentered the house, and climbed the stairs. He tiptoed into Sarita's room and leaned over to kiss her. "*No, hombre,*" she protested, drawing the blankets to her forehead. "Your nose is like an igloo."

"You mean icicle."

"The same."

"I'll be back before sunrise. Jesse, too." He went to the door.

"Mark?"

"Yes."

"It's just a tree. Nothing has to grow from it."

"Is that what you want?"

"I don't know."

He shut her door, and awoke the boy.

"Now?" Jesse asked. "Why can't you go yourself?"

"Because I'm snow blind," said Mark, laughing.

"What's that?"

"When you know where you're going, but can't see the way there."

Downstairs, Mark warmed some milk and tucked Jesse's pant cuffs into a second pair of socks before the two laced up their ski boots. He put a thermos of hot chocolate, extra mittens, and a small folding saw into his pack.

It was new to Jesse: the squeaking hardness of the soft powder underfoot; the clapping and clacking of the sticklike box elders overhead, shaking free their slight burdens of snow; and the drum-like roll and thud of tall drifts sliding off the barn roof as the two skiers glided past. From a fence post an owl screeched at them and startled Jesse. Mark's heart also beat wildly.

After a mile they turned north, climbed several hills, and from the highest saw the tree farm below, where rows of pine tops bobbed above the thick snow like strings of dark beads. Buoyed by the deep powder, they skied fast and effortlessly downhill, and through the jammed open and partially buried gate.

Jesse picked a good one and they made quick work of taking the tree. Shuffling back under the arched gateway, the boy flicked a ski pole so quick and high at the overhang that he caught Mark off guard, showering his face with snow. Jesse howled with delight, then pointed overhead to the now exposed wrought iron sign that the snow had hidden. "Brandon Brothers Tree Farm," he read. Mark stopped. The excitement he felt only a moment ago was gone. He put the tree down.

"What are you doing?" said Jesse.

Mark jabbed at the sign with his pole. "I know these people."

"You said that there was no one. Nobody owned it."

"I thought it was abandoned. And it may be so. Thing is, Eddie Brandon tried to give me a tree in town yesterday. He got ticked off when I said no."

"But wouldn't he want you to have one then?"

"I don't know," said Mark. "Wanting to give, and then having the same thing taken from you are different." Giving was satisfying, he thought. It repeats, and redeems the gift of life. Taking undermines all that.

Jesse turned his skis so that he faced Mark. "Let me explain to you, *Señor Serioso,*" he said, barely able to contain his glee. "We can't exactly glue it back on now, can we?" The two skiers laughed heartily.

"Eddie Brandon, this be the one!" Mark shouted into the stillness of the night. "Thank you for keeping me in your prayers."

He threw a chunk of snow at Jesse, who nimbly ducked underneath it.

Mark lashed the tree to his ski poles to carry over his shoulder. He and Jesse switchbacked up the big hill, traversing and kick-turning until, reaching the tall pines, they could look out toward the great lake and see below all the farms and orchards nestled in the checkered folds of the snowy woods. The climbing was difficult—all the more so without the use of his poles—and though Mark's lungs burned, wood smoke from someone's hearth sweetened the cold air. Above them the stars stretched from horizon to horizon.

The wind picked up, so they took shelter behind a copse of pines bent in half by the weight of snow. Mark set the tree down, poured the hot chocolate, and the two skiers removed their sodden mittens to warm their hands on the steaming cups. Mark told Jesse there was probably more snow overhead in these trees than on the ground in the cities downstate. He pondered a world that winter made smaller, humbler, and more primitive. Snow redeemed the fallowed land, made the harsh angles—the frozen, mudded ruts in the road, the downed limbs in the apple orchards, the debris of errant hunters—soft again, and skis were wings to explore it.

Jesse thanked him for the best hot chocolate ever, dropped under the snowy boughs, and pushed off.

Mark tightened the small tree to his poles, shifted the weight over his shoulder and, steadying it with one hand, followed. Soon he heard the soft parade of deer moving into the swamp below. Living in the country, he often saw or heard what others—Sarita and Jesse, even—had to imagine. Then, too, he thought, at times—serious times—he was only able to imagine what they saw plain as day. Christmas, for example. Family.

Mark skied Jesse's tracks along the ridge, and then followed them down, down, leaning back on his heels so the tree wouldn't slip forward and cause him to catch his tips in the snow. He gained speed, faster and faster, finally slinging past the boy—only to skid to a stop near a candescent figure on the windblown crust at the edge of a cornfield. Jesse caught up and he, too, stared at the peculiar shape the wind and snow had slashed and carved and fused of withered stalks the combine had missed. Starlight danced in waves across it.

"What is it?" asked Jesse.

A freak of nature, thought Mark. Its single trunk and sweeping columns looked familiar, like a remnant from his past that, inexplicably, the storm had uprooted. Then he knew. "A menorah."

"A what?"

"A menorah. It's how my family—my people—honor their past. Lighting candles. Singing songs." Mark stared at the candelabra-like object that glowed between them until he started to shake. It was a festive holiday, he thought; had he forgotten that, too? And yet, away from the temple—skiing the dunes and woods—he had never felt closer to it. *But closer to what?* The question nagged at him. God was never his thing. Yet he undeniably felt closer and closer to…as if he were sliding downhill and couldn't stop the approach to something he had no name for. It pulled at him, this uneasy connection, like the pull of a former lover, the string never severed. He thought God was maybe that. A string without end.

Jesse knocked the ice from his skis with his pole. Mark wanted to say something that the boy would remember. "My father wanted to be a cantor," he blurted, as the tree fell to the ground.

"What's that?"

"A priest, sort of. Who sings."

Jesse shifted his weight to his stronger leg. "You don't celebrate Christmas."

"No." Mark stood the tree upright in the snow next to the candelabra.

"But why not, you know, be part of it? We're all people."

We're all people, thought Mark. Skiing the black holes, jumping from star to star. Skating the thin ice. "A long time ago, there was a fork in the road," he said at last. "The path my people took led me here."

"My mom says the past is past."

Mark laughed. His mother had told him that the past will never let you forget. "This is different," he said. "What I'm saying is, I can't go a way I've never been. I'd miss out on where I was. Who I am."

"So Christmas makes you feel, I don't know, like you turned the wrong way or something?"

"Yeah," said Mark. "Lost."

Jesse put his hand in Mark's, as much as his pole let him. "That was fun. I never skied like that. Didn't think I could do it."

"I never thought I could either," said Mark. He reached into his pack, got the scraper out, and shaved the ice from their ski bottoms. "We've got to move, or our skis will ice up," he said.

"I don't get it," said Jesse, not going anywhere. "You get both—" he pointed to the tree and bundle of stalks. "And celebrate neither." He smiled at his own cleverness. "What do you believe, anyway?"

"That the sun will soon rise, as it should. So we'd better get going, get the firewood in and put the tree up."

What did he believe? That the earth embraced the sky. Simple. He believed in the stars and dreams and in certain waxes for certain days. He believed in magic where snow fell from a cloudless sky, and in castles made of ice stacked along the shore of the big lake on a sub-zero day and in the waves that made them and erased them and crashed over them to freeze in midair and shatter like glass. He was wet and chilled to the bone and it didn't matter. He believed that, too.

They were almost home: a last hill to traverse, then down and along a tangle of new growth where they'd find their old tracks. At their side, a few corn stalks not buried in the snow fluttered in the wind, and to the west, a black tongue of cloud welled up over the lake to swallow the last of the stars. *The darkness behind the light.* It would snow again.

AKNOWLEDGMENTS

I am indebted to three editors whose vision, clarity, and encouragement helped move these stories along: John Mauk, then with the Michigan Writers Cooperative Press, for his initial readings, patience, and advice; Katey Schultz, for her selfless compassion and wisdom; and Tanya Muzumdar, for her ongoing support and sensibilities.

ABOUT THE AUTHOR

B.L. Makiefsky spent his formative years living an itinerant life that included picking cherries in the Hood River Valley, harvesting hemp in Iowa, working construction in California, reporting news in west Michigan, crisscrossing the country on a motorcycle, hopping trains, and hitchhiking. Since the initial publication of *Fathers and Sons*, his work has appeared in several literary magazines and journals. For a listing of the author's other work, go to blmakiefsky.com.

Other titles from Michigan Writers Cooperative Press:

The Grace of the Eye by Michael Callaghan

Trouble With Faces by Trinna Frever

Box of Echoes by Todd Mercer

Beyond the Reach of Imagination by Duncan Spratt Moran The Grass Impossibly* by Holly Wren Spaulding

The Chocolatier Speaks of his Wife by Catherine Turnbull

Dangerous Exuberance by Leigh Fairey

Point of Sand by Jaimien Delp

Hard Winter, First Thaw by Jenny Robertson

Friday Nights the Whole Town Goes to the Basketball Game by Teresa J. Scollon

Seasons for Growing by Sarah Baughman

Forking the Swift by Jennifer Sperry Steinorth

The Rest of Us by John Mauk

Kisses for Laura by Joan Schmeichel

Eat the Apple by Denise Baker

First Risings by Michael Hughes

Fathers and Sons by Bruce L. Makie

Exit Wounds by Jim Crockett

The Solid Living World by Ellen Stone

Bitter Dagaa by Robb Astor

Crime Story by Kris Kuntz

Michaela by Gabriella Burman

Supposing She Dreamed This by Gail Wallace Bozzano Line and *Hook* by Kevin Griffin

And Sarah His Wife by Christina Diane Campbell

Proud Flesh by Nancy Parshall

Angel Rides a Bike by Margaret Fedder

Ink by Kathleen Pfeiffer